But What If I Don't?

Jessi Abell

But What If I Don't?

ISBN 978-1-79476-601-3

A NOTE FROM THE AUTHOR

In the end, whether you finish it or not,
put this book down, and pick up your Bible.
The only book that will truly answer your
questions was written thousands of years ago.
Only the Shepherd can bring you out of this valley.
This is just the story of a sheep who's been there.

PREFACE

"But what if I don't?"

I can still remember the exact moment when I heard those words slip down from Heaven. I was trying desperately to hold myself together in a mustard-hued Ronald McDonald House bathroom in Atlanta, and I was failing miserably. How did I end up here? What part of following God faithfully since the age of seven had resulted in such an unimaginable fate? How did I go from growing up in church, leading Bible studies, and marrying a youth pastor to begging for my child's life between a towel rack and an old tub? It wasn't supposed to be this way. I wasn't supposed to be here. But I was.

Every bit of religious dogma I had picked up over the years burned up and melted away in the heat of desperate reality. It was just me and God, wrestling for my sanity on that cold, tile floor. Only a day after bringing my daughter into the world, I was pleading with God to heal her. Surely, He would. I knew He could.

"I know you can heal her God! You are Jehovah Rapha! God my healer! You are great! You are mighty! You are able!

I *know* You can heal her!"

"But what if I don't?"

BEFORE

Everyone comes from somewhere. Everyone has a story. Every smile, every frown, every wrinkle, and every scar is the result of something. Some combination of experiences - added to our DNA, temperament, family dynamic, and the divine orchestration of it all - contribute to who we are. We have all grown up somewhere, been raised by someone, experienced things both good and bad, and made choices that we love and regret. We have all seen things, heard things, learned things, and taught them to others. We have things we love and things we hate for reasons all our own.

That stranger in the grocery store, the girl at the gym, that kid that sits in the front row of your classroom, and the old lady from church are all uniquely crafted people who have experienced things you will probably never know anything about. And until you know where they have been, it's hard to understand where they are. Why they are the way they are. Why they do what they do and say what they say. This book is deeply personal to me, so if you are going to read it, you may as well know a little more about who I was before that fifth night in January.

I grew up short, shy, and Baptist. I was a pretty standard product of a small South Georgia town. I made a lot of good grades and a few great friends. I played the flute, sang in the choir, and had little athletic ability. I was in church anytime the doors were open, and sometimes when they weren't, because I had a key on my ring as soon as I could drive. I went to all the kid's camps, and when I outgrew them, I lead them. I was immersed in Bible drill, Sunday school, youth ministry, and mission trips, and for that, I am forever grateful.

When I graduated from high school, I went to a small college about an hour away and met the man I would eventually marry. I still remember the first time I saw him. I was sitting in an honors class of about twelve people, and we were going around doing one of those awkward 'first day of class' introduction activities. We each shared our name, along with our primary life goal. Can I tell you that I have NO recollection of what my primary life goal was at that time? But I do remember his.

His name was Zach, and right there in front of peers he had never met, he stated his goal: to spread the gospel of Jesus Christ. I was floored. Don't get me wrong, I had aced Sunday school. I knew that was the right answer. But for him to be that bold in the real world took guts. And what can I say?
I noticed :)

Fast forward a few months. We had been dating for a few weeks when he invited me to go to church with him. Thinking nothing of it, I agreed. Later that week, he picked me up, and on the way, he asked if I had ever been to a Pentecostal church. I thought it was a strange question since everyone in Southern Georgia was obviously Southern Baptist like I was. But in the spirit of conversation, I entertained his question and replied, "No, have you?".

Cue one of the most interesting evenings of my life.

Within the hour, I found myself in the midst of a service the likes of which I had never seen. No "order of service" was printed because, come to find out, no one knew what was likely to happen so, why waste the paper? I was accustomed to a church where the preacher stayed behind the pulpit, the prayers were soft and scheduled, and the loudest portion of the service was the carefully planned moment after the first hymn and before the announcements where you were encouraged to shake your neighbor's hand. Things were a little different here.

Here, the people moved around during worship. They danced, they jumped, they walked about. The pews were more of a place to sit and take a break rather than a permanent residence. And prayer was now apparently a group activity. In my experience, a group prayer consisted of standing in a circle, holding hands, and praying one at a time, squeezing the hand next to you when you'd finished, so they knew it was their turn. Here, everyone just prayed all at once - a real time saver actually. And don't even get me started on the altar call. As a newly certified lifeguard, I came incredibly close to performing CPR on a lady I assumed had fainted from some sort of ailment. Rookie mistake. I would later realize that this was business as usual. So much so that there were blankets on hand to cover anyone who was out for very long. Considerate.

I had to reconcile a lot of differences as I floated between the different denominations, spending many nights pouring over the Word and seeking out truth. I challenged my new boyfriend on nearly every point of his faith, an experience which I believe truly grew us both. I learned a lot during this time, but it all really boiled down to one thing: God does not fit in a box.

As people, we like to understand things. We like to set rules and get a handle on how something works. But the reality is, you just cannot get a handle on God. You cannot predict Him. You cannot control Him. You cannot contain Him. He is all-powerful, all-knowing, and all-present. And dare I say, He does not align Himself with one denomination over another. He is beyond religious practices and procedures. He is GOD, and He does not fit in a box. I did not know it then, but coming to this realization shored up my faith's foundation so that it could withstand the approaching storm.

A few years later, I married that boy. And two years after that, we brought a sweet and spunky baby girl into the world. We named her Emma Grace. When Emma was two, we bought a house in my hometown where my husband was newly employed as a youth pastor. We were settling into a regular life of raising a family and ministering to teenagers when we found out we were expecting another baby girl in January. Emma was as elated at being a big sister as a two-year-old could be. We organized the nursery and washed the baby clothes. We decorated. We planned. But God had plans of His own. As we prepared to hold our baby, He prepared to hold us through what would be the most difficult season of our lives.

DURING

When my Addie was born, we were blindsided. Instead of holding a sweet, newborn baby girl, counting toes and figuring out whose nose she had, we watched as she was loaded onto a helicopter bound for Children's Hospital of Atlanta. Immediately, we were flooded with calls and text messages, "How is she?" "How are you?" "What is happening?" "How can I pray?" In an attempt to keep everyone informed, we started a Facebook group. In hindsight, the entries from that group tell her story pretty well -

January 6, 2016

On January 5th at 5:03 PM, we welcomed little Addison Beth Abell into our lives. She is 7lb 15oz of beautiful baby girl :) Unfortunately, Miss Addie was born with some complications. This page exists to keep friends and family up to date on her condition as she fights to get better. Thank you for your prayers as we trust God in this day by day.

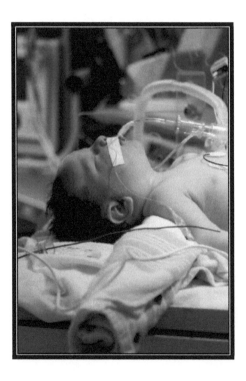

Looking Back

As I'm writing this, I realize that unfamiliar readers may benefit from an explanation of Addie's condition, known as a Congenital Diaphragmatic Hernia. CDH's occur in about one in every 2,500 babies per year. This condition arises when the baby develops a hole in their diaphragm, the muscle that separates organs in the abdomen from organs in the chest. In some cases, it can be detected prior to delivery through ultrasounds. But little Addie just wasn't ever at the right angle when her ultrasounds were done. At some point prior to delivery, some of her intestines and other abdominal organs found their way through the hole in her diaphragm and became lodged in her chest cavity. This put immense pressure on her lungs and pushed her heart way over to the side. Thanks to some incredible doctors, she was diagnosed soon after delivery, and we were all sent to Children's Healthcare of Atlanta.

January 7, 2016

Addie and Zach have been in Atlanta since Tuesday evening, and I've been here since Wednesday. Since her admission, Addie has been put on a treatment called ECMO (extracorporeal membrane oxygenation). Basically, this machine places oxygen into her blood so that her little lungs get a break. She'll be using this for at least a week. Once she's taken off ECMO, she will undergo surgery to get her intestines back down in her belly and repair the hole in her diaphragm. So, for now, we wait, and watch God work. Thank you all for your concern and your prayers. This is a big deal, but our God is so much bigger!

Looking Back

This entry seems simple enough. What you don't see here is the struggle that went into getting us to Atlanta. This was not the plan, and we had another small child who was too young to visit the NICU wing of the hospital where her little sister now lived. Our family literally could not be together. We had to leave Emma at home with grandparents (and thank God for them!) while we stayed in Atlanta with Addie. I missed my baby girl's first day of preschool so that I could be at her little sister's bedside. No matter where I was, I always felt like I needed to be somewhere else. There simply was not enough of me to go around, and it broke my heart. I remember this time in my life, and am so grateful for our incredible parents stepping in to take care of our oldest. And I am so indescribably proud of our little Emma being so brave while we were away. But it kills me that she went through so much of this time without me there.

Addie is doing well on the ECMO right now, so the plan for the weekend is to just maintain where she is and let her little body heal and strengthen. Next week, we will start discussing gradually pulling her off the ECMO. After she is off, we can plan for surgery on her diaphragm to correct the hernia. We still don't know exactly what the condition of her left lung is, and probably won't until they can do the surgery. So prayers are still and always will be greatly appreciated.

Looking Back

I can still smell the soap. Every single time we entered the NICU wing, we had to wash our hands at a special sink with a certain antibacterial soap. I can still smell it to this day. Just like I can still see the rows of beds with inconceivably tiny humans on them, and hear the almost constant humming and chirping of monitors. NICU life is like nothing else you'll ever experience. You feel essential and yet completely useless at the same time. Your child is fighting for their life, and you can do absolutely nothing but sit, and watch, and wait. So that's what you do. For days, you sit in a chair and watch your baby breathe. You pray. You read. You try to make small talk with the nurses and technicians as if you aren't living your worst nightmare. You struggle to put on a brave face and ask good questions when the doctors round, even though you're constantly fighting tears and can't remember your last shower. It's a time warp, where minutes turn into hours and hours slip by into days. Sometimes nothing changes for weeks. Sometimes your world changes in a second. It's mind numbing and heart wrenching, and you just don't get it until you get it.

January 11, 2016

It's hard to simply answer the question 'How's Addie?'. In appearance, she's beautiful. Her color is perfect, her cheeks are chubby, and her eyes are deep blue like her big sister's. If you can look past all of the machines, she is gorgeous. In spirit, she's feisty. The nurses keep her full of sedatives in an effort to keep her as still as possible. But our Addie is a fighter. She's constantly scrunching her little nose, waving her tiny hands, or wiggling her perfect baby toes. She's going to be a handful :) Medically, the doctors say she's average considering her condition and her time on the ECMO machine. Things change by the hour as one number goes up and another level goes down. It's a lot of sitting and waiting and praying. We don't have any definite dates to look towards. It all depends on little Addie. Please continue to pray that she'll be able to rest and grow stronger as we hope to take her off ECMO and move on to the surgery to fix her insides. She's a tough little girl, but she needs all the prayers she can get. Thank you all so much!

January 20, 2016

We can't possibly thank everyone enough for your continued prayers. We have seen God's hand at work in so many ways. Addie is improving, but we're reaching a point where some specific things need to happen soon. Addie is finally becoming less dependent on her ECMO machine. To put it in perspective, she started at a 50, and has to make it down to 20 before she can be taken off. After a lot of back and forth, she's currently at 31. The troubling thing is that her machine is wearing out. It's only meant to be used for about two weeks, and tomorrow makes two weeks for Addie. If they have to replace the machine, we lose all the progress Addie's made. And while she's made some strides, a setback like that could take a serious toll on her. Please be in prayer that Addie will continue to wean off the machine quickly, and that the machine will hold up long enough for her to do so. It's a tall order, but our God is able. We can't thank you all enough for joining us as we seek His will and His strength for our baby girl.

At 11 AM this morning, Addie's doctors 'capped' her ECMO machine. Basically, they turned it off just to see how she'd do without it. Folks, that was over two hours ago and she still looks great!!! They're keeping a close eye on her, but our baby may be ready to come off this thing! Prayers are being answered! Please keep lifting her up in the coming days. The machine won't last through tomorrow, so we need her to truly be ready to come off. Thank you all so much for your prayers! God is so faithful. He's getting us through this one step at a time!

Looking Back

As I'm writing this book and remembering this time in particular, I feel there are some things you should know. First, the entry you just read was written on a Sunday, and that particular Sunday morning was the first time we'd attended a church service since Addie's birth. You should know that it felt impossible to be anywhere but her hospital room at such a critical time, but we went anyway. And you should know that God moved mightily for our Addie while we worshipped Him. We literally received the call as we were walking out of the church that Addie's ECMO had been capped and her vitals were holding steady. We had to hurry back to the hospital so that we could witness the miracle God had been working out while we were gone. Never underestimate the power of difficult worship.

January 27, 2016

We have a surgery date! This Friday morning, somewhere between 9 and 11 AM, Addie will have the surgery that we have been waiting for from day one. It's another huge milestone, and another scary obstacle on her road to getting better. Please be in prayer as our tiny girl faces this enormous event. Specifically, please help us pray that the pulmonary hypertension she's developed will improve when her little insides get straightened out. Thank you all again for standing with us through this battle. We have seen the power of prayer demonstrated so clearly as we have watched our baby girl overcome one day at a time. Please continue praying! We have come so far, and we have a ways to go.

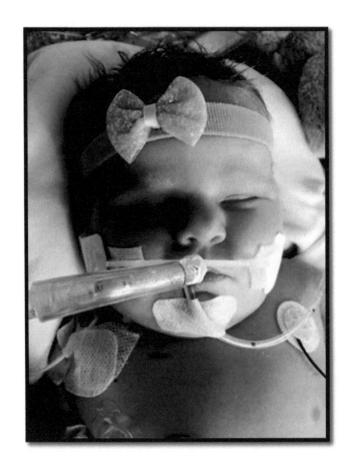

Addie's first bath, first bow, and first surgery date planned.
Its been a big day!

Sweet dreams world!

<u>**January 29, 2016**</u>. (Surgery day)

Thank you all so much for your prayers!!! She's a tiny girl with a big boo boo, but she made it through surgery like a champ! Everything is in its rightful place, and her lungs are already looking better. She had no hypertension issues during surgery, which was a serious concern. The doctors and nurses are so in love with her, and continue to be impressed with her tenacity. She's a beautiful little fighter with the power of prayer behind her. Right now, she's resting back in her comfy NICU bed, getting the royal treatment for the next few days as she heals. To God be the glory for bringing us this far. He's carrying us through this valley one step at a time!

Looking Back

"They cut her in half!" I remember saying this to Zach the first time we saw Addie after her surgery. Her incision was no more than a couple of inches long, but it might as well have been a foot in my mind. Nothing can prepare you for seeing your child go through something so monumental, especially when there is nothing you can do to help. Reflecting on it now, though, I am reminded of how God carried me, and her, through it all. I couldn't do anything to help my girl in those hours, but God could do it all. He was, is, and will always be in complete control. What solace we can take in that!

He promises in His word to never leave or forsake us (Deuteronomy 31:6). This doesn't promise us a life of ease, but is an assurance that GOD WILL BE THERE through it all. He is always present, always intentional, and always in control.

February 3, 2016

Little Addie is steadily weaning off her ventilator and pain medication. She is receiving food through a feeding tube and handling it really well so far. Please pray with us that her tiny tummy will be able to digest the increasing amounts of food she'll be given. She has to work up to eating a certain amount, and we have been told this can be a long process.

I realized earlier that our Addie will be a month old on Friday, It's truly amazing to look back over her life so far.

<u>29 days ago:</u> Addie was born, but not breathing. She was immediately flown to Atlanta, and our journey began.
<u>27 days ago:</u> Addie was placed on ECMO. We were warned that this was incredibly dangerous, but it was necessary to save her life.
<u>10 days ago:</u> After spending 17 days on a machine that should have only lasted a couple of weeks, Addie was taken off ECMO. This was another

risky but necessary procedure, and she came through beautifully.

5 days ago: Addie underwent the surgery We have been waiting for her whole life. It was extensive, but again, she came through wonderfully! We were cautioned that she would have some challenging days after surgery, but instead she has steadily improved,

3 days ago: We held our baby girl for the first time!!

And today: Zach changed a dirty diaper :)

It just goes to show what God can do in a month!

Thank you all AGAIN for your prayers! Our baby is living proof of what God will do when His people pray.

February 9, 2016

A baby's cry is recognized everywhere as a sign of life and health. It was the first thing we listened for when Addie was born, but we were met with terrifying silence. For over a month we watched our baby lay quiet as a machine pumped air in and out of her lungs. The most we ever heard was a squeak as the ventilator pushed air by her vocal chords. But no more! As of yesterday, there's another crying baby in the Egleston NICU!! Little Miss Addie is off the ventilator and breathing on her own! And there is absolutely no denying that it's all thanks to God hearing His people pray. One

of my favorite worship songs says:
"It's Your breath in our lungs, so we pour out our praise! We pour out our praise!"
Nothing brings that song to life like knowing your child's every breath is a direct answer to prayer. This experience has made us so aware of God's presence in the simplest of things. Every heartbeat, every breath, every cry. It's all by His grace and for His glory. What a mighty God we serve!

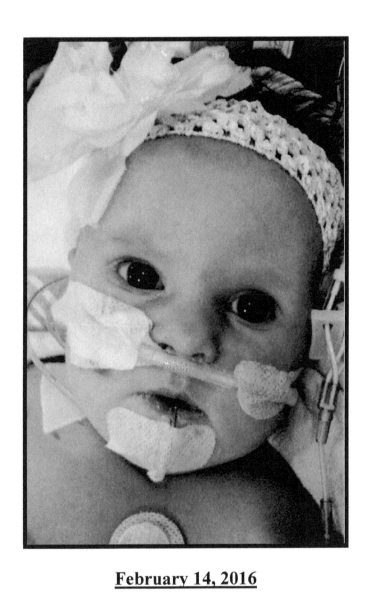

<u>February 14, 2016</u>

Happy Valentines Day!

Love, Addie

February 15, 2016

We spoke with Addie's doctors this morning, and there is no doubting she has come through some incredible things in the last 40 days. Even so, they made it clear that Addie still has a long road ahead before she can come home. We're basically looking at three obstacles. She has to be able to tolerate a certain amount of food, breathe completely unassisted, and be weaned off of her hefty dose of pain medication. These are all slow processes, and even more so when combined. Our baby is going through a lot right now and will be for a while. God has brought her through so much already. Please help us pray for progress as He continues writing her story.

March 4, 2016

Sorry folks, this is a long one.

We learned this morning that Addie has developed a staph infection from her incision. The good news is that the doctors caught it early and are confident that they can treat it with a week of antibiotics. The not-as-good news is that she'll be in isolation for the rest of her stay. This means a secluded room along with gloves and gowns for all of her nurses. This obviously wasn't our plan, but we know that God is in control. He's brought her through so much already.

I spoke with Addie's doctor this morning and asked for specific prayer points. If Addie's journey has taught us anything, it's that God does wonders when His people join in prayer. She answered with three things:
1- That Addie's pulmonary hypertension would continue to improve. Her heart has been under a lot of stress in her short life, and that has made it tougher than it should be.
2- That her breathing would continue to strengthen. Though she's breathing on her own, she still requires some support.
3- That her staph infection will not worsen or spread, but will heal quickly and completely.

We know God is able to heal our baby. He's already brought her so far, taught us so much, and touched so many. Please join us in continuing to seek and trust His will for our sweet girl. May every challenge serve to bring Him glory!

March 8, 2016

There's nothing like watching God answer prayers! Three days ago, I asked Addie's doctor for specific areas to pray over. She answered with three: Addie's pulmonary hypertension, respiratory support, and her newfound staph infection. Now, three days and lots of prayers later, God is showing off through baby Addie :) Her last heart echo showed improvement in every aspect of her pulmonary hypertension. She's been steadily, even aggressively, weaned on her respiratory support and is thriving. And last night she got her final dose of staph antibiotics, and her incision looks fantastic! Today they'll remove her pic line (the bunch of IV's in her left arm), and they may even try bottle feeds! It's all good news! It's been amazing to watch God work in so many ways! Surely, He has big plans for this baby girl. Thank you all so much for your continued prayers!

"For everything there is a season, a time for every activity under heaven." Ecclesiastes 3:1 (NLT)

Waiting is hard. Waiting to finally bring your baby home can feel impossible. Little Addie will be ten weeks old tomorrow. For ten weeks We have been running this race, watching God pull our baby over one hurdle at a time. It's been an uphill road, but He's been faithful every step of the way. This weekend, Addie was moved to the 'B side' of the NICU. This is where the most stable babies are cared for before they go home. She's doing so well, and she's been brought so far, but she's got a few stubborn obstacles between her and the door.

The first is her feeding. With all she's been through, every bit of food she's ever had has come through an IV or a feeding tube, and the sucking reflexes she was born with have become dull. The doctors are working now to help her learn to take a pacifier and bottle, but it's a tedious process. Addie is having to gradually learn what comes naturally to most babies. If she can pick it up and begin taking her feeds by mouth, it will be a huge step! The second and most serious is her medication weaning. They're going painstakingly slow, but she's still showing symptoms of withdrawal. Few things are more difficult than watching your sweet baby girl struggle through such a grown-up problem. Every time she has to go back up on her dose, it sets her back another day or two. It's a balancing act between keeping her comfortable and weaning her completely.

God's plans are not our plans. His ways are not our ways. And His timing is not our timing. But they are better. We know He has purpose in every obstacle and in every day. For everything there is a time, and this is our time to wait. Please keep praying with us as God continues to work in and through baby Addison.

March 26, 2016

We're in the home stretch! At least, we might be. A few days ago, Addie was taken completely off her oxygen. She's now breathing room air, tube free, just like any other baby! Her medication is weaned enough for her to finish it out at home. Also, she's taking all of her feeds through an NG tube, meaning her stomach is doing all the work. This is something they're fine with her coming home on. So we're close! We're so so close! The only possible issue is that she's lost a little weight due to all of her digestive issues. If she can turn it around and start steadily putting on weight again, we're talking DAYS until we get to load her up and bring her HOME!! Please help us pray that this sweet little chunk can put on some weight. I've already threatened to sneak some Hershey's syrup into her feeding tube...but hopefully it doesn't come to that ☺

March 31, 2016

It seems our baby girl has just a few more lives to touch in Atlanta before she heads home. Due to some incredibly bad reflux issues, little Addie is going to be the proud owner of a GJ (gastrostomy-jejunostomy) tube. This means her formula will be pumped into her stomach via a small tube in her side. She'll have the procedure next week, and about a week after that, she'll head home :) Life will look a little different than we planned, but We have learned that man's plans don't matter much in the long run anyway.

In C. S. Lewis's 'The Lion, the Witch, and the Wardrobe' a girl asks if Aslan the lion is 'quite safe'. Laughing, her friend tells her 'Course he isn't safe! But he's good'. How true this is of God. If you're following Him expecting it to be easy, you'll be sadly disappointed. Our God is not a God of 'easy' or 'safe', but He is always *always* good. He doesn't keep us from the valleys, but He does lead us through them. He has purpose in every step. Every trial, every challenge, every victory, every breath has purpose when we follow His lead. So, as we face this bump in the road, we won't be discouraged. Instead we'll glance over our shoulder at the mountains God has brought us over, and know that He's got this too.

'Come and see what the Lord has done...'
                              Psalm 66:5 (NLT)

Let me brag on my God for a minute. The scan on the left (next picture) is of Addie the night she was born. Everything was in her chest. Her heart was pushed way out of place, and the doctors weren't sure if she even had a left lung because it was covered by her intestines. It was a mess. A terrifying mess. But God was just getting started. Flash forward 3 months. The scan on the right is Addie's most recent X-ray. Both her lungs look fantastic, her heart is back in the middle, and everything is where it should be. The doctors say you'd never know she was born with half a diaphragm. Now here we are with just one more day. That's all that stands between us and the door! Barring anything crazy, our baby will finally come home Wednesday! For the first time in her 3-month life, she'll feel the fresh outdoor air, ride in a car seat, and finally meet her very anxious big sister. And we are so ready. Well, mostly. Between now and then, Zach and I will learn to run a feeding pump, administer meds, and manage a GJ tube. Caring for her will be a lot different than we'd imagined, but we count it as a privilege. Throughout Addie's stay we have heard nurses, doctors and specialists of all kinds refer to her as a 'miracle baby'. God has truly blessed us with this sweet girl and charged us with the unique task of raising her. Parts of it are overwhelming, but none are as incredible as the work God has done in her life, and will continue to do as she grows.

We started this journey broken. Shattered. All our plans and preparations were worthless in the face of this storm. Organs were misplaced, the future was uncertain, and there was absolutely nothing we could do but rely on God. And so, we did. Now, 14 weeks later, He has restored order to the chaos. He has healed what was broken. And He has brought us so much closer to Himself in the process.

If I've learned anything from this, it's that God never abandons His children. You will go through the valley at some point. That part isn't optional. But if you're following God, He'll be there to catch you, and He'll guide you through. And when you get to the other side, you'll look back and say 'Come and see what the Lord has done!'

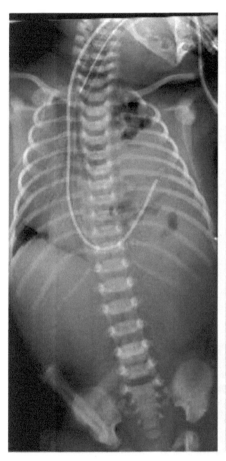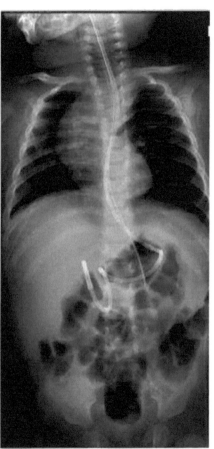

<u>April 13, 2016</u>
A big bow for a big day
We're headed home!

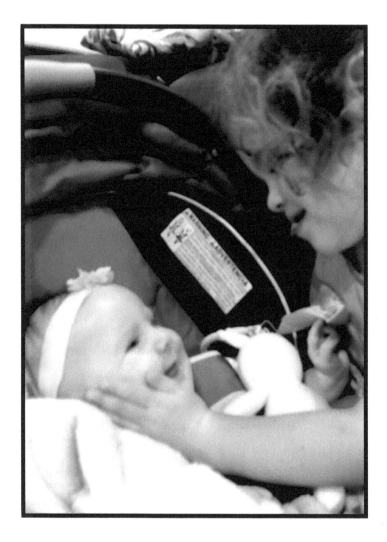

<u>April 14, 2016</u>

These two have waited three long months to meet each other. I'd say it was worth it :) (Easily one of my favorite pictures of all time!)

May 20, 2016

Evening folks :) I originally planned on the last update being the very last update. Prayers were answered and we were coming home! But the thing is, that was only the beginning! Every day is an adventure around here. Addie still hasn't gotten the hang of a bottle, so for now she is on a GJ tube. For twenty hours out of the day she's hooked up to a pump which gives her a gradual flow of formula. We're working every day to get her to take a bottle, but she's a stubborn one. Somehow, I don't mind :) Don't get me wrong, life with a baby on a feeding pump isn't easy. You wear a backpack everywhere you go. You're constantly mindful of the cord dangling around your feet as you carry your baby. Every movement is a dance...'don't step on it, don't get tangled in it, don't get it caught on anything...'. And there are countless concerns that don't come with a 'standard' baby. I can tell you exactly how many milliliters of formula my child has every hour (51 as of yesterday, just in case you're curious). The cord wasn't something we planned on, and I'll be thrilled to see it go! But I don't hate it. It's a reminder of where my brave baby girl has come from. What she is still overcoming by God's power and grace. Every time I get tangled up in that dumb cord I stop, I breathe, and I smile. Because at the end of that dumb cord is a chunky little miracle :) Her therapists and doctors keep going on about how social she is. She smiles at everyone as if she knows how precious

her days are. And maybe she does. I know I do.
Thank you all for praying for our baby. This
chubby little smile is for you!

May 31, 2016

"Though He slay me, yet I will hope in Him"
Job 13:15 (NIV)

Never have I identified so closely with Job.

Visitation will be held Wednesday June 1st from 6-8PM at Cobb Funeral Chapel.

Her funeral will be Thursday June 2nd at 2PM at Lakeside Assembly.

Thank you all for everything

AFTER

Looking back...

There just aren't words. Things were fine, until they weren't. We were settling into our new normal as a family with two beautiful girls and a feeding pump. Therapy appointments, adjusted milestones, joy in the struggles. Things were fine. Things were good. Until they weren't.

My husband and I had gone out to dinner for the first time since bringing Addie home. But our dinner was cut short when my parents called to let us know that Addie was spitting up and seemed ill. Once again, we made the late-night drive to Atlanta, where Addie had spent her first four months of life. We spent the weekend there while her doctors searched for any issues that may be causing her reflux, but they didn't find anything. We brought her home on Sunday afternoon, and settled in to rest up for Memorial Day lunch at my parents' house the next day.

That Sunday night, my girl hit another milestone. She rolled over in her crib! I was so proud, but also completely terrified that she would get tangled in a cord or pull her feeding tube loose. So I sat up with her. I spent that entire Sunday night rocking my sweet baby girl. I held her in my arms and sang all those songs I had sung to her in the NICU when I wasn't sure if she'd ever come home. I took in her deep blue eyes and stroked her soft chubby cheek as she drifted off to sleep in my arms. It was such a small moment. At the time, I'm sure I was tired and wishing I could get some sleep. But looking back, its one of my most treasured memories. God was so good to have my sweet girl roll over that night.

The next day, we went to my parents' house for Memorial Day. My mother and I sat and talked on the front porch, enjoying the beautiful weather. I sat on the ground while Mama rocked with Addie in the porch swing, All at once, we realized that Addie had stopped breathing. She never fussed or fought or gave any indication of pain. She simply drifted off. The ambulance came. They did everything they could. But man's efforts are nothing in the face of God's plans. She was gone.

Why?

As the mother of a two-year-old, I hear this question constantly. Swiftly following nearly every instruction or statement, a tiny little voice questions 'Why mommy?'. Sometimes I explain things in painstaking detail because I want my girl to understand. But sometimes the answer is a simple 'because mommy said so baby'. It's not because I love her any less that I don't explain. Nor is it because there isn't a reason. But if my baby girl asks me why the sky is blue, I'm not going to launch a complicated discussion about molecules and light reflection. She would never understand. Instead I tell her that's just the way God made it. In times like these, when nothing makes sense, my Heavenly Father reminds me that there is purpose in the pain. Though it is far beyond our understanding, He has a plan. I may never know the reason, but I know my God. And I trust Him. I thank him that my sweet little Addie no longer has to fight to breathe, or depend on a tube to eat. She is whole and healed and perfect, snuggling in the arms of her heavenly father. And when it hurts, I'll remember her tenacity. She smiled in spite of everything, and so will we.

Looking Back

One thing I learned quickly as a grieving mother was that no two people handle grief in the same way. If you're in this place, please be patient with yourself. There is no right or wrong here.

. For days, I could hardly stand to go into Addie's room. The blanket where I'd last changed her diaper laid on the floor untouched. Her empty crib glared at me from beneath the wooden letters on the wall that spelled her name. It wasn't' that long ago that Emma helped me paint those letters in preparation for her little sister's arrival. And now she was gone.

Finally, I decided to do something. Some may think its crazy, but it was right for me. I took a deep breath, and through hot tears, I began to take that crib apart. I'm not much of builder, so it was a clumsy process, but I knew this was what I needed to do....

One of my favorite stories in scripture is in the book of Acts. Paul and Silas had just been beaten and thrown into prison for casting out a demon. They were in pain from what the Bible calls a 'severe flogging'. They were in the dark, because they'd been placed in an inner cell. They were likely cold and naked because the magistrates had ordered that they be stripped before they were beaten. So there they sat in the pitch black of midnight, in incredible pain and shackled to the wall. And in the face of all that was wrong in their lives, they sang hymns and prayed....

I thought of Paul and Silas that day as I worked on Addie's crib. I'm sure they didn't feel like worshipping based on their circumstances, but they did it anyway. They turned that prison into a sanctuary. They took a place of sorrow and made it into a place of praise. Their songs of exaltation mixed with the groans of pain from their wounds as they worshipped in their prison cell. They created an altar in the most impossible of places.

And I would do the same.

For months after she left us, I used Addie's crib as a prayer desk. I literally sought God in the most impossible of places, and it made my walk with Him so much stronger. If you're familiar with the story of Paul and Silas, you know that it doesn't end in that prison cell. As they sang songs of praise and prayed to God in Heaven, the earth beneath them began to shake. The very foundations of the prison that held them captive began to tremble, and the door to their cell was flung open, allowing them to walk right out of what was once inescapable.

And we can do the same.

There is power when we choose to praise in the prison, and make altars out of the impossible places in our lives.

August 24, 2016

"Look now; I myself am he!
  There is no other god but me!
I am the one who kills and gives life;
  I am the one who wounds and heals;
    no one can be rescued from my powerful hand!"
                    Deuteronomy 32:39 (NLT)

This isn't the most popular verse in the Bible. I imagine it's because we don't want to acknowledge that death and wounds are as much a part of God's plan as life and healing. We fervently pray for what we feel is the best outcome, and are shattered when it doesn't happen. We have this feeling that God dropped the ball. If only He cared more, loved me more, heard my prayers, then He would have succeeded. But the thing is, He didn't fail. He never does.

Soon after we lost Addie, I heard a message from Tim Hines in which he advised: 'If your situation seems impossible, try to see it as God sees it.' Finding myself at the most impossible situation of my life, I took his advice. And this is what I saw...

1- God had every opportunity to take my baby to Heaven while she was in the hospital. ECMO, surgeries, even a staph infection. At one point she was given a 30% chance of pulling through. He helped her overcome so much. And against all medical odds, she came home! She slept in her own crib. She was held by her grandparents. She went to church. And best of all, she finally met her adoring big sister face to face.

2- When it was her time to go, she didn't do it surrounded by machines and doctors as she had lived so much of her life. She slipped away softly in one of her favorite places, being rocked by her grandmother on a beautiful back porch. She always loved being outside...

3- She passed on Memorial Day. This may seem a small detail, but it isn't. Any other day, Addie, Emma, and I would have been home alone all day. But on Memorial Day, everyone was off work and we'd gathered together for lunch. She was surrounded by family, and we were all there for each other. I can't imagine going through that time on my own.

It was always God's plan for Addie to leave us when she did. He did not fail. Her every moment was precious to us and to Him. When you look at her life and even her passing, His fingerprints are everywhere. It still hurts every day in ways that words can't describe. And it probably always will. But I take heart in knowing that God did not forget me. He didn't lose interest or stop caring. He is every bit as present and intentional in taking as He is in giving. We have only to look hard enough.

January 5, 2017

Today is not what I'd imagined. There will be no colorful balloons. No brightly wrapped presents. No messy little hands or cake covered face. So many things are different, but one thing hasn't changed. Today is a day to celebrate you.
Your strength in spite of frailty
Your joy in spite of pain
Your determination in spite of impossible odds
As long as I live, I'll never forget the look on your face every morning. You greeted each new day with wide eyed wonder and a big toothless grin as you looked up at me from your crib. You truly were thankful for every precious moment you had. In spite of every struggle you endured, you met each sunrise with hope and anticipation. May we all learn to be that way.

May we be so enthralled with the potential of what God can do with each new moment, that the troubles of this world simply pale in comparison. May we resolve to see the good when the bad threatens to blind us. May we sift through our pain to find the lessons God has for us. May we seek joy that passes understanding rather than fleeting happiness. May we love when it doesn't make sense. My sweet, strong, precious baby girl. You taught me so much with that smile. I'll love you forever.

Happy Birthday.

May 19, 2017

"Praise be to the God and Father of our Lord Jesus Christ, the Father of compassion and the God of all comfort, who comforts us in all our troubles, so that we can comfort those in any trouble with the comfort we ourselves receive from God." - 2 Corinthians 1:3-4

This is a tough one.

The pain of losing a child is inconceivable to those who haven't experienced it. It's simply beyond words. When I lost my baby, I didn't just lose her sweet chubby face or her precious monkey toes. I lost a lifetime. I will never get to plan her birthday parties, attend her graduation, or dance at her wedding. All I'll ever plan for her is her funeral. There will be no 'first day of school' outfits, no prom dresses, no wedding dress shopping. The last thing I ever chose for her to wear was the lace dress she is buried in. I'll never pick flowers in the yard with her like I do with her big sister. The closest I'll ever come is selecting flower arrangements for her grave. We aren't meant as people, as parents, or as mothers, to bury our children. It's an impossible task and an unbearable pain. The one shred of comfort I found in the days following her passing was the knowledge that she was finally healed. She was free of every medical issue or worldly care. Her only thought was of her Heavenly Father's glory. Her every moment was filled with dancing and singing His praises. She was finally free to worship.

Ironically, that was the one thing I simply couldn't do. As a Christian, I knew that I had to seek God even in the midst of this struggle. I remembered the words of Job, when he said of God 'though He slay me, I will hope in Him.' I poured myself into Bible study, prayer, and seeking God in the middle of the chaos, because in the words of Peter, 'where else could I go?' I could talk about Him, read about Him, even pray to Him. But I could not worship Him. Not after what He'd allowed to happen. Not after what He'd allowed me to go through. I knew that in this world I would have trouble, but God had crossed a line. The pain was too much. The anger was too strong. The bitterness weighed heavy in my heart, and any time I started to approach the throne room, I was overcome by resentment toward my God. How could He?? Finally, in a fit of rage and pain, I came charging at God, fists clenched, anger blazing, without a shred of reverence. I brought every ounce of bitterness, anger, blame, depression, and doubt that I had and threw it into His face. At the end of my rope and at a loss for fancy prayers, I cried out to God, 'How could You ever expect me to truly worship You? You've put

me through more than I can bear! You have asked too much of me, the pain is too great! God, You don't understand, I watched my child DIE!'
And as the dust settled, I felt God softly say, 'So did I'

God CHOSE to watch His son die an unimaginable death to pay our debt. And why? So that we could have a relationship with Him. So that we could pray to Him. So that we could WORSHIP. We take our salvation for granted because it comes freely to us, but we forget that it cost the God of the universe everything. He CHOSE to send His son to the cross. He didn't have to do it, but He did. And yet we come to His house, sit in our seats, and wait to be entertained as if He owes us something. We cling to our pain, anger, bitterness, depression, and hurt, as if having a difficult life excuses us from worshiping our God. Like His glory can be outweighed by our pain. Like His worthiness depends on our satisfaction. As if His holiness is determined by how obedient HE is to OUR will. We have become so confused! He paid the dearest price conceivable to open the door to us, and yet we would sit on the steps as if it wasn't enough.

HOW DARE WE?

We sit and wallow in our doubt. We tell God 'I just don't understand'. We wait for God to explain Himself before we submit to Him. But we forget that we were never called to understand, we were called to obey. To bring God glory. To worship. In the book of Job, God allowed a man to be put through every imaginable hardship. And when Job confronted God, he wasn't told 'why', he was told 'who'. In one of the most awe-inspiring chapters of the Word, God reminds Job of who He is, of what He's done, and of the glory He is due. God doesn't address Job's complaints. He addresses Job's perspective. And once it is corrected, worship ensues. God does not owe us an explanation. And we have no obligation to understand. He is worthy of our worship because of who He is, regardless of our circumstances. Our worship doesn't have to be pretty. And if you're going through the valley, it certainly won't be easy. But I can guarantee you, you'll never find the purpose behind your pain by holding onto it. Your identity is not found in your wounds, but in your healing. I know it can feel impossible to come before God when we're hurting, but it's the only way we'll ever see the other side of it. God didn't allow pain into your life to stop you, but to grow you. You have to keep going! Your purpose is not in your circumstances, but in your lineage. We are children of God, no matter what happens, and He does not abandon His children. Worship doesn't have to be pretty, but it does have to happen. Because God is God, and we are not.

Now, when I draw near to God in worship, it still isn't easy. I am never more aware of my scars than

when I praise the One who healed them. My God
and I have been through the fire, and the journey
isn't over. But when I truly draw near to my God,
and I praise Him simply because He is worthy, I
am always reminded that I am not alone. There are
so many things my Addie and I will never do
together. But when I raise my voice to God, I
know that it joins hers.

In worship.

To understand the following, you need to know that God blessed us with the world's cutest baby boy on July 1, 2017. We named him Noah. We had the name picked out before we ever had a child, but it was so much richer now. Noah, a man of extraordinary faith, who built a boat in the middle of the desert, simply because God said to. A pillar of trust in God's faithfulness, whose perseverance saved the human race according to God's grace. It was a sweet reminder of God's eternal promise to be with us, even in the midst of life's storms. Our Noah reminded us of God's faithfulness in so many ways, as you'll see in the next entry...

September 26, 2017

Sometimes God shows His enormity in the tiniest of ways. Knowing that two of my children will never meet this side of Heaven has been hard, but God's fingerprints are still there. On the left is a picture of Addie's scar from her diaphragm repair. On the right is a picture of my 3-month-old son, Noah. See that tiny birthmark on Noah's belly? It's in the exact same place as Addie's scar. It could have been anywhere. He didn't have to have a birthmark at all. But he does. And it's there. In that exact spot. I know this is a small thing, and some would argue it's only coincidence. But to this mother's heart, it means everything that, though he will never meet her here on earth, my sweet Noah will carry a God-given reminder of his precious big sister. Such a tiny thing for such a big God to concern Himself with, and yet He does.

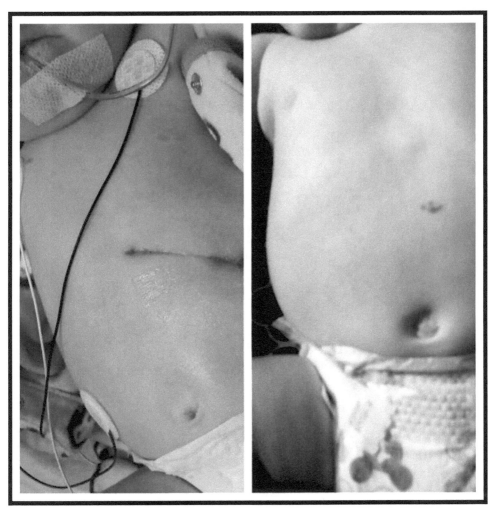

Addie   Noah

January 5, 2018

"As the heavens are higher than the earth, so are my ways higher than your ways, and my thoughts than your thoughts." - Isaiah 55:9

Today my Addie would be two years old. Walking, talking, and playing Barbies with her big sister. I often think about what might have been, but find comfort in trusting that God knows better than I do. Just as Heaven is a better place, His plans are better plans. If Addie were here, she'd have a cake and balloons. We'd sing happy birthday and blow out her candles. She'd get presents from her loved ones and be made to feel like a princess.

But His plans are far better.

Instead of cake and balloons, she has her place in a heavenly mansion. Instead of the happy birthday song, she is surrounded by angels singing choruses of praise to the Lord. And rather than receiving gifts like a princess, she gets to give her worship to the King of Kings in His very throne room. Things would be different if she were here. But I know that His ways are far better.

Still, sending some balloons can't hurt.

God has used this season to teach me some truths that have become invaluable in navigating life after loss. I share them with you in the hopes that they may help you get through whatever valley you find yourself in. Just as parents communicate with their children in different ways, according to their temperaments, God speaks to us in many ways. To me, He tends to use images and metaphors that may or may not make sense to everyone else. I'll share them in faith and hope they reach someone who needs them.

FORGIVING GOD

I know the idea of forgiving God is theologically incorrect. But if we're being honest, its one of the first things I remember struggling with after we lost Addie. I don't love the thought of working through this publicly, because the last thing I want to do is mislead anyone. But after a lot of prayer, I feel that this book would be incomplete without addressing this feeling. I am not a theologian. Nor am I one for rocking the boat or causing debates. If the idea of 'forgiving God' puts a knot in your stomach or a check in your spirit, please feel free to skip this part. I'll never know. But if you've struggled with that feeling that God has wronged you in ways that man never could, and the subsequent guilt that follows admitting to such a thought, I wrote this part for you:

Let me begin by saying that I know without a shadow of a doubt that God is perfect by His very nature, and that He doesn't make mistakes. I know that He doesn't need our forgiveness. He never does things that are wrong. But sometimes He allows things that hurt.

Usually when you hear about forgiveness, it's in terms of forgiving another person for a wound inflicted, be it intentionally or by mistake.

Sometimes it's even about forgiving ourselves. In either case, the lesson normally boils down to the fundamental issue that man is sinful and will inevitably let you down at one point or another. But I had no human person to hold responsible for losing my baby. When Addie died, every single person involved was doing everything within their power to keep her alive. The doctors were excellent. The ambulance drivers were exceptional. There were three people present that day, myself included, who knew CPR, and we were all there doing everything by the book. People worked. People tried. People prayed. But God made the call and took my baby home.

God. Not man.

So how do you navigate that?

I'm drawn again, as I was soon after Addie's passing, to the story of Job. Here is a man who did everything as correctly as any man could. He sought God, obeyed God, and even made sacrifices to atone for any possible sins of his children. He was not at fault when his life was decimated before his eyes. His wealth, his family, and even his very health and well-being were stripped from him by no fault of his own. But when he challenged God to this effect, he was not met with some sort of explanation or apology, because God was not in the wrong. God stepped forth and reminded Job, as

He would us, that He is creator and, therefore, owner over the foundations of the world and everything that has come about since. (Job 38:1-18) Everything. Every place and every person were made by Him and ultimately for His glory. God reproves Job for suggesting that He explain Himself, leading Job not to a place of forgiving God, but of repenting himself. Job later receives worldly rewards far beyond what he lost, but his true reward is the same as ours when we pass through a time of deep suffering. To exchange the need to forgive God for an awareness of His unwavering perfection even in the midst of great trial is to go from merely hearing God to seeing Him. (Job 42:5) Our suffering is not an opportunity to forgive God, but to recognize His authority over ALL things, even those we hold most precious, and to repent of our skewed perception of Him.

>>>---------- >

"As arrows in a quiver are the children of one's youth" - Psalm 127: 4

While my Addie was in the hospital, a sweet cousin of ours gave us a onesie for her to wear. It was made of simple white cotton, and written in gold were the words 'Though she be but little, she is fierce'. And underneath those words was a golden arrow. Throughout her life, that onesie became a treasured reminder of my baby girl's inner strength. Through all of her physical ailments and shortcomings, she was strong and fierce. She didn't let her outer circumstances taint her sweet and innocent spirit. She had a goofy little smile for every person she met, even though many of the people in her life came to her with shots and painful procedures. She greeted them with an open heart and happy expectancy. She didn't judge people based on her past experiences. She accepted them with joyful abandon, not because of what they'd done to her in the past, not because of who they were, but because of her own inner God-given strength to face the future and look ahead to the possibilities it may hold. If only we could all live our lives that way!

While she was here, that simple arrow held so much meaning. It reminded me that though she was frail like a slender arrow, she was oh so strong and capable of incredible things. Every sweet smile in the midst of tubes and machines bore witness to the strength within her. After my sweet Addie passed, the arrow began to take on a new meaning to me. You see, an arrow in and of itself isn't really strong at all. Its long, narrow, and could be easily broken if left to its own defenses. An arrow on a shelf is hardly worth fearing. An arrow on the ground could be broken by any passerby. Oh, but an arrow in the hands of a skilled archer…now that is a different matter entirely. I began to realize that I was facing my life's most difficult season. Grief, doubt, anger and resentment all weighed heavy on me, ready to snap me in two. On my own, I would surely break, as an arrow on a shelf. It was only by placing myself in God's hands that I would be able to remain strong. This life brings so much hardship in one way or another. We all have different stories, different struggles, and different ways of handling things. But there's one thing we have in common: without God, we will break. It's that simple. We are all arrows, terrifyingly fragile if we try to go it alone, but capable of incredible things if we only submit our will to the Father. If we allow our experiences to sharpen us, and our God to direct us, we can go from being a frail twig to a fearsome weapon. An arrow is only as strong as the archer who holds it. Who's holding you?

FAITH

I've heard it suggested time and time again that if we only have enough faith, then anything is possible. If we pray hard enough, fast long enough, and believe fervently enough, our requests will be met. We just have to keep pushing and pleading and standing and claiming and holding on, and if we can just believe hard enough and long enough, it'll happen. We just have to have faith.

Can I tell you what immense guilt that places on the mothers who have lost children? Did we just not pray hard enough? Or what about believers whose illnesses remain? Is their faith just not strong enough? What about men and women of extraordinary faith who have prayed for something and not seen it come to pass? Is it somehow their fault? I was struggling with all of this one day when God led me to a few different passages. I'd read them all before, but they came alive in a new way now. Never let anyone tell you the Word of God is stale or outdated. It is as living and true today as the day its words were penned.

In John chapter 9, we read about an encounter between Jesus along with His disciples and a man who'd been blind since birth. The disciples asked Jesus plainly who had sinned and caused this man to be blind? They boldly and unashamedly assumed that this man's loss of sight was a result of someone's wrongdoing. I wonder sometimes if the man heard them. Being blind since birth, he'd made his way in the world by listening to what was around him. How many times must he have heard those who passed by speculate at his expense? "What must he have done?" "Must have been something awful!" "Do you know his parents? It's no wonder he's blind". People assumed that his circumstances hinged entirely on his actions. But Jesus knew better. He answered His disciples, saying 'Neither this man, nor his parents sinned. He was born blind so that God's works may be revealed in Him'. It wasn't the blind man's fault that he was blind. He was given a testimony planted in hardship and brought forth by an encounter with the Lord.

The Bible also speaks of Paul. A man of God by any standard, Paul was afflicted with something he called a 'thorn in the flesh'. Scholars have speculated for years over what it was exactly, but that isn't relevant. The point is, this mighty man of God prayed in earnest not once, not twice, but three times that God would take this thorn away. But God left it. Whatever it was, Paul's prayer for its removal was not answered in the way that he asked. He didn't receive the result he asked for, but he continued to serve God as resolutely as ever, because his faith was not in the result, it was in God.

Sometimes our prayers are not answered in the way we would like. Loved ones pass, difficulties persist, and illnesses continue. If this is the case, we should remember that we are in good company. On the night of His arrest, Jesus himself prayed desperately, 'Father, if You are willing, remove this cup from Me, yet not My will, but Yours be done'. You can almost see the flesh and spirit in Jesus colliding as he uttered these words. His flesh pleaded for His own will, that He would be spared the incredible pain of unjustly dying on the cross. Yet in the same breath, His spirit overcame as He submitted His will to God's. He had undeniable faith, but it wasn't placed in the outcome of His prayers. It was placed in the One He prayed to. He begged God to make another way. But we know that later that night, Jesus was taken and soon after crucified in a selfless sacrifice for humanity. Jesus prayed so hard that He sweat drops of blood. He lived a life completely without fault, and we know that He had undeniable faith. Throughout His life, He performed miracle after miracle and healing after healing. But in this case, at this point, when He prayed perhaps the most fervent prayer of His life, God chose another way. Jesus submitted His will to that of God in Heaven, and as a result, He saved all of Creation.

Faith is important, but its placement is crucial. Sometimes we are so determined to have strong faith that we forget to seek first the One we have faith in. If His will is different from ours, as it may well sometimes be, then we have to know Him well enough and trust Him deeply enough to have faith in Him even then.

A WET INDIAN

What defines you? If you're like me, it can be easy to begin to label yourself according to what you've been through. I'm a mother who has lost a child. Somehow letting my life revolve around anything other than that fact felt like a betrayal of my baby girl. Like if I wasn't in a constant state of grief then I was moving on. Letting go. Forgetting her. I was wading through all of this one morning on the way to church when God hit me with a metaphor. It's odd, I know. But it made all the sense in the world to me, and maybe it will to you too.

'IF AN INDIAN FALLS INTO A LAKE, HE IS A WET INDIAN. BUT HE ISN'T A FISH'

Here's what I took from it. If an Indian is walking along, and by some turn of events happens to fall into a lake, he will be affected. He will be wet. His clothes will be soaked. He will walk differently due to the discomfort. He will be more aware of approaching bodies of water. He will look at ponds differently than he did before, and empathize with others who have also fallen in. His life view will change. He will forever see and feel things differently than he once did in the light of his experience.

He will be a wet Indian. But he will not be a fish.

Our experiences CHANGE us.
They AFFECT us.
But they do not DEFINE us.

Regardless of what we have been through, our identity lies in Christ and there alone. Losing Addie has been the hardest experience of my life, and it has changed nearly everything about me. It has altered my perspective, my opinions, my relationship with God and with others. My life has and forever will be changed, but my identity remains the same. I am loved by God.

On the good days, I am loved.
On the bad days, I am loved.
When I grieve, I am loved.
When I rejoice, I am loved.
When I doubt, I am loved.
When I run away, I am loved.
When I come home, I am loved.
When it all falls apart
When it doesn't make sense
When everything has changed
When I can't depend on anything
Still, and forevermore, *I am loved.*
And so are you.

And that should give us joy! It should give us peace and assurance. Those things aren't a denial of our experiences, but a grateful acknowledgement of God's undying love for us, and our unchanging identities in Him. I don't know who you are, what you're dealing with, or how you're handling it all. But if I could offer a word of encouragement, it would be this: God hasn't changed. Neither has your identity in Him. So feel your feelings. Miss your loved ones. Mourn for what makes you sad. And then rejoice in the fact that these things may affect you, but the love of God alone defines you.

You may be a wet Indian. But you are not a fish.

EVERYONE HAS A TEN

"Please pray for me! This test has me so stressed out!!!"

This is a Facebook status I read on one of my first nights in the Ronald McDonald House. We had just come back from a day in the NICU of Children's Hospital of Atlanta to get a few hours of sleep. Down the street, my days-old child was hooked up to goodness knows how many machines and monitors. Addie had just been placed on ECMO, a machine that removes the blood, oxygenates it and puts it back in the body, which is every bit as scary as it sounds. Her heart was struggling. We weren't sure if she even had a left lung. Her every moment was a fight to stay alive. Meanwhile this kid wanted prayer for their testing anxiety.

I was livid at this poor person who I barely knew! How dare they ask for prayer, ACTUAL prayer, for their 'super stressful' test? A silly little test! They had no idea what real stress was! My baby wasn't breathing on her own and they wanted ME to pray for THEM? I didn't know it at the time, but this irrational anger would become an ongoing battle for me. For the longest time after Addie passed away, I had difficulty empathizing with those struggling around me. Any time anyone shared a trial, a testimony, or a prayer request, I was filled with resentment.

'You want prayer for what?? You have no idea what real pain is...'

At this point, I imagine most of you think that I'm a truly terrible and heartless person, and I can't blame you. I know this mentality sounds harsh. But if you've been through something tough, you may relate. And if you do, you should know that you aren't alone. If showing my ugliest side helps you realize you aren't on your own in this, then it's worth it. That said, this was really out of character for me! Since I was young, I've always been a 'put yourself in their shoes' kind of girl. But having gone through something like the death of a child left me feeling calloused to the struggles of others. It wasn't until God got my attention that my perspective finally changed. I was listening to someone relay the details of some life struggle they were experiencing, and as I felt the familiar wall of resentment rise, God demolished it with a simple thought:

"THIS IS THEIR 10.
IT MAY NOT BE THE SAME AS YOUR 10.
BUT IT IS STILL THEIR 10."

When a doctor asks you to describe your pain, they'll often ask you to do so on a scale from

1-10. 1 is no pain at all, while 10 is excruciating. Unbearable. The worst. I realized I had been measuring everyone else's experiences against my own. And if I felt that it didn't measure up, I dismissed them. But their 'worst', their 10, was still their 10, even if it wasn't the same as mine. It really hit home on a new level after discussing the whole thing with my husband. He's always good at drawing parallels between the physical and the spiritual. I suppose that's one of the perks of marrying a youth pastor. After confiding with him about this particular issue, he said something simple but profound:

'Isn't it amazing that after all Christ went through, He still empathizes with us?'

Wow. That hit me square in the pride. Here I was, sitting on my pain pedestal, acting as if my experience gave me any right to measure everyone else's. Meanwhile, Jesus Himself, who died for the very ones who killed Him, draws near to the hurting every day. He encourages those who are tired and heavy laden to come to Him, that they may find rest.

Who was I to judge where Jesus justified?
Even on His way to be crucified, Jesus stopped and wept, not for Himself, but for the people He would die for. I pray that God would take my pride and replace it with a heart like His.

One that isn't blinded by my own pain, but rather drawn to the hurting, bringing honest compassion to a world that so desperately needs it.

TREES AND WEEDS

Look to the oak, so mighty and strong
It's trunk so stout, it's branches long
It's highest leaves dance in the clouds
It's roots stretch deep as it stands proud
But it wasn't always so

For had you been here in the past
You would have seen just dirt and grass
Though now it stands so proud and tall
This oak began quite weak and small
Many years ago

It started life as just a sprout
Breaking earth and peeping out
It needed sunlight, longed for rain
This tiny oak had much to gain
It had so far to go

The sun, it shone. The rain, it fell
The oak, it grew. But not too well
For the sun and rain met all it's needs
But what fed the oak also fed the weeds
And so, they too, did grow

The weeds grew fast and thick and tall
The sapling oak was still so small
They blocked the sun and caught the rain
And caused the oak such awful strain
Yet still, it strove to grow

The sun, it shone. The rain, it fell.
The oak, it grew. But not too well
The sun and rain met all it's needs
But what fed the oak still fed the weeds
And so, they too did grow

The struggle lasted days on end
Days and weeks and months...but then
A wise old farmer happened by
He'd seen this happen many times
He said 'Young oak, you have your needs
But what's fed you has fed these weeds'
And He began to sow

Then one by one, He pulled them out
He killed the weeds and freed the sprout
But as the oak was freed at last
It felt such pain shoot from the past
It's roots were tangled so

The weeds so tall, their roots so strong
Had wrapped the sprout up far too long
They'd grown as one and shared its needs
What fed the oak had fed the weeds
But now they had to go

And free at last, that oak, it grew
It flourished then with strength anew
And now the clouds, it's branches stroke
For what fed the weeds, now feeds the oak
And heavenward it grows

(Trees and Weeds cont.)

When we go through the worst of things, they have the potential to grow 'oak sized' faith. But that faith begins as just a sprout. As the sun and rain of difficult circumstances feed our faith, they also tend to grow 'weeds' of anger, self-pity, unforgiveness, doubt, depression, and a host of other hinderances. Left to ourselves, we can't have one without the other. What feeds the oak will also feed the weeds. What could produce unconditional trust may create doubt. What could produce incredible joy may instead lead to depression. What could produce monumental purpose may instead bring about a lifetime of self-pity. We are only saved from these weeds of sinful reactions by the power of God. He alone can remove these things from our lives, but it's rarely an easy process. The weeds of life that would choke out our faith are oftentimes rooted in hurt, and removing them can prove to be a painful experience. But it is necessary if we are to encounter the oak of faith that God has planted in our lives and nurtured through adversity. Friend, if you are stuck, tangled in weeds of unforgiveness, anger, bitterness, depression, please hear me. I get it. I've been there. But you have to know that that dying sprout of faith is still alive, and could soar to the clouds if only you would let God remove the weeds surrounding it. Adversity is one of God's greatest tools in growing faith, but we MUST get the weeds out of the way.

PURPOSE OVER VALIDATION

Grief is an odd thing. It's a common experience with the most uncommon and unpredictable results. I fully believe that two people could encounter the same tragedy, in the same way, at the same time, and emerge with completely different reactions. To measure your own response to a tragic event against someone else's is to set yourself up for undue confusion and self-doubt. So I would encourage you, even as you read this, to be patient with yourself and with God as you journey through this time. Look for His unique purpose for you and you alone. God is not a God of 'one size fits all' experiences. What you are facing, feeling, and fighting is not in vain. But we must seek God's purpose rather than the validation of others if we are to find true peace and ultimate healing. Hang in there friend. Grief is one of God's richest journeys if we only have the strength to hold fast to Him.

BUT WHAT IF I DON'T?

It's the question God asked me at the beginning of this journey in that Ronald McDonald House bathroom. I wrestled with it then, because it implied something impossible. That question suggested that a good, perfect, and loving God might give me a beautiful baby girl, only to take her away. And how could I possibly contend with that? But looking back, as ridiculous as I know it must sound, I am grateful.

Yes. Grateful.

I am grateful for the certainty that this has brought to my life. I know now, beyond even the shadow of a doubt, that the God I claim to follow is truly, completely, and forevermore my one true God. My relationship with God is my everything. My sustenance. My faith is not a hobby. It's my very breath and bread in every single season. My God is not an ideal, He is my rock. My foundation. My fortress in time of greatest need. And I can say all these things now with the highest level of certainty because they have been tested. I can stand alongside Job, knowing that when God tests me, I can come forth as pure gold (Job 23:10). And that certainty is priceless. In a world obsessed with the here and now, we forget how fleeting our time on earth is. Every person, every race, every status, every nationality has but one thing in common.

One day, sooner or later, we will face death. It's the thread that unites all of humanity and yet we ignore it and sweep it under the rug, distracting ourselves with more 'pressing matters' like wealth and beauty. We walk so willingly into a trap set by the enemy, answering all sorts of questions: What do you want to be when you grow up? What do you do for a living? Where do you live? How much do you make? What makes you happy? What are your goals? What have you achieved? But we forget the most important one. In fact, the only one that matters: Where are you spending eternity? Because in the grand scheme of things, this life is a breath, a shadow (Psalm 144:4) And the highest highs and lowest lows one can possibly experience within its bounds can't hold a candle to the potential of eternity. The single most important thing we have to accomplish in this life is establishing a real, authentic, enduring relationship with God.

Not a hobby. Not an ideal. A relationship.

Just like Aslan in 'The Lion, The Witch, and The Wardrobe', God is anything but safe, but He is good. In a way that no worldly distraction can be. Nowhere in His word does God promise a life of ease and comfort to those who choose to follow Him. What He does promise is His presence, that He will never leave or forsake His children. In the best and worst of times, He is faithful.

So the question remains, where does your faith lie? Is your faith based entirely on what God has done in your favor, or do you trust in God Himself? Do you trust Him for who He really is, or do you trust the idea of an all-powerful, well meaning, loving and doting father-ish being so long as things go relatively well for you?

If you've been through the worst this life has to offer, then you know that there is nothing that can sustain you through a storm but the love and faithfulness of an unfailing God. If you've leaned on Him, you've found shelter. If you've sought refuge somewhere else, you've been disappointed. Or you will be. Losing Addie has undoubtedly been the most difficult experience of my life. There are still days when I buckle under the sheer weight of it. But in the midst of grief, I am grateful. Yes. Grateful. Because I know now that the faith I have in my God will not be shaken. And in a world full of false hope and temporary treasures, that certainty is invaluable. It is peace in the face of chaos. It is love in the face of hate. And it is joy in the face of suffering. I have an unwavering foundation because it is built on God's character and not on my circumstances.

When He acts in my favor,
and if He doesn't,
I will follow Him.